The Light of Life
In the Spirit of Man

The Light of Life
In the Spirit of Man

by
Charles Capps

HARRISON HOUSE
Tulsa, Oklahoma

4th Printing
Over 23,000 in Print

The Light of Life
In the Spirit of Man
ISBN 0-89274-470-7
Copyright © 1987 by Charles Capps
P. O. Box 69
England, Arkansas 72046

Published by Harrison House, Inc.
P. O. Box 35035
Tulsa, Oklahoma 74153

Contents

1

God Wants
to Light Your Candle

You are important to God. Though darkness is all around today, God has made provisions for you so you won't have to walk in darkness.

The same God Who commanded light to shine out of darkness wants to turn the light on inside you. He wants to enlighten your darkness. Let's find out how He is going to do it.

Therefore hath the Lord recompensed me according to my righteousness, according to the cleanness of my hands in his eyesight.

With the merciful thou wilt shew thyself merciful; with an upright man thou wilt shew thyself upright;

> With the pure thou wilt shew thyself pure; and with the froward thou wilt shew thyself froward.
>
> For thou wilt save the afflicted people; but wilt bring down high looks.
>
> For thou wilt light my candle: the Lord my God will enlighten my darkness.
>
> Psalm 18:24-28

David says, **For thou wilt light my candle: the Lord my God will enlighten my darkness.** The Word says if you walk in darkness you know not at what you stumble.

The Human Spirit — God's Light Bulb

Proverbs 20:27 says, **The spirit of man** (the human spirit) **is the candle of the Lord, searching *all* the inward parts of the belly.** This is not talking about the stomach; it is referring to the human spirit.

The spirit of man — the human spirit — is the candle of the Lord. In the day these scriptures were written, candles were used for light; but modern man doesn't think of a candle as a light. Today we would say it this way: "The human spirit is the light bulb God uses to enlighten you."

Your Bible may have a footnote that uses the word *lamp*. The spirit of man is the *lamp* of the Lord, searching all the inward parts of the belly.

The word *belly* is used in both the Old and New Testaments, usually referring to the human spirit. Jesus, when talking about the Holy Spirit, says it this way: **Out of his *belly* shall flow rivers of living water** (John 7:38). He was speaking of the Holy Spirit which had not yet been given.

When you receive the Holy Spirit, He dwells within your human spirit for God's Spirit bears witness with our spirits. Concerning things of the spirit, the Apostle Paul admonishes us to compare **spiritual things with spiritual** (1 Cor. 2:13).

In John 4:24, Jesus says, **God is a Spirit: and they that worship him must worship him in spirit and in truth.**

Created in God's Image

God Who is a Spirit created man in His image and likeness. In the beginning, He said:

> **Let us make man in our image, after our likeness: and let them have dominion over the fish of the sea, and over the fowl of the air . . . and over all the earth.**

> Genesis 1:26

Adam was created to be ruler under God and have dominion over all the earth. God didn't intend for man to be a little worm in the dust, searching for things to do and not knowing how to do them. He gave man dominion over all the earth.

Man was to function in that realm because his candle was lit. His spirit was like God's, for it came out of God. He was in God's likeness.

God breathed into Adam the breath of life. (Gen. 2:7.) *The Amplified Bible* says He breathed into Adam the *Spirit of life.* God breathed *His Spirit life* into man, and man became a living spirit being made in the image and likeness of God.

I believe Adam was an *exact duplication of God's kind*.

What *kind* is God? God is a spirit.

Since God is a spirit, we cannot contact Him with our bodies. We contact Him with our spirits. There are angels around us, but we cannot reach out and get a handful of angels. They are spirits and do not have physical — flesh, blood, and bone — bodies.

Several years ago, I was teaching in a certain church about understanding the human spirit and how we communicate with God through our spirits. I made the statement: "Spirits communicate with spirits, not with physical bodies." Suddenly, a CB radio broke in over the PA system and a voice said, "Hey! What are you-all doing down there?" Three men jumped up and ran in three different directions! I thought they were leaving, but I found out later that they were running to turn down the PA system. It almost made their hair stand up, like mine, but it did put the point across.

Spiritual Light and Revelation

God is a Spirit. He must be worshipped in spirit and in truth. He uses your human spirit to enlighten you, to bring revelation and understanding of things you don't know naturally.

You can be a highly educated, intellectual person and have no spiritual understanding. Your carnal mind may be educated, but your spirit may be uneducated concerning the things of God. As Paul said, **The natural man receiveth not the things of the Spirit of God: for they are foolishness unto him: neither can he know them, because they are spiritually discerned** (1 Cor. 2:14).

The Book of Isaiah states: **When the enemy shall come in like a flood, the spirit of the Lord shall lift up a standard against him** (Is. 59:19). Since the Holy Spirit has been given and we are living under a new and better covenant, I believe we should read it this way: "When the enemy comes in, *like a flood the Spirit of the Lord shall lift up a standard against him.*"

Where does this flood come from? Jesus said: *Out of your belly* (your spirit) **flows rivers of living water.**

When you know not how to pray as you ought, the Holy Spirit *helps* your infirmities, or weaknesses. (Rom. 8:26.) What does the Holy Spirit do? He sheds light and gives insight to your spirit when you don't know how or what to pray. Then He makes intercession through your spirit in the perfect will of God. This is spiritual light that God brings to you, the revelation that comes through your human spirit when your candle is burning.

Supernatural Insight

There is no way we can understand all the things God moves upon us to do or say. I have had people to call or write me from hundreds of miles away and say, "What were you doing on a certain day at a certain time? I was led to intercede for you, and I prayed in the Spirit." When I checked my calendar, I found that they were right on! I was in need of prayer at those times.

One winter, at the exact time they were praying, I was flying in bad weather and flew into freezing rain. My airplane began to take on a load of ice. I did need prayer — their prayers! The Holy Spirit knew my need and revealed it to their spirits. They didn't know how to pray effectively in their natural language; but because their candles were lit by the Lord, they had light in their spirits to pray in the perfect will of God.

The Word Brings Light

David said it this way: **The entrance of thy words giveth light** (Ps. 119:130). So God's Word brings enlightenment to the spirit.

Now let's look at John 1:1-4.

In the beginning was the Word, and the Word was with God, and the Word was God.

The same was in the beginning with God.

All things were made by him; and without him was not any thing made that was made.

In him was life; and the life was the light of men.

In him was life. In *who?* In the *Word* (Jesus). In *the Word* was life, and the life was the light of men. This is why David said, *"God will send His Word and light my candle."* The entrance of the Word brings light.

In Psalm 119:105 he said, **Thy word is a lamp unto my feet, and a light unto my path.** The Word is a lamp or candle that enlightens darkness. The Word entering your human spirit enlightens your darkness!

I don't believe we have fully recognized the wisdom that is released in the Word of God. Wisdom comes out of the mouth of God; it is His Word revealed and conceived in the human spirit. Wisdom comes by the Word of God and thrives in the human spirit.

The wisdom of the Word affects everything you do and say. It will give you light when darkness is all around. While others are wringing their hands, not knowing what to do, the Word *conceived* will bring you light.

Someone might ask, "What part do I read to get the wisdom of God?" The answer is simple: *all of it!* You can get healed on the begats or gain wisdom just listening to genealogies!

Saturate yourself with the Word of God. Get the New Testament on tape and play it day and night in your home. Give yourself to the Word. The *entrance* of His Word brings light.

You might say, "I just don't understand how that would bring light to me." It will because it *is* light and it *is* life! Jesus said, . . . **the words that I speak unto you, they are spirit, and they are life** (John 6:63).

The Word affects your total being. It will cause you to make correct decisions and not know why you made them. It will bring healing to your physical body. **He sent his word, and healed them, and delivered them from their destructions** (Ps. 107:20).

When this says God sent His Word, it means exactly that. Jesus was the personification of God's Word: **And the**

Word was made flesh, and dwelt among us (John 1:14). **In him was life; and the life was the light of men. And the light shineth in darkness; and the darkness comprehended it not** (John 1:4,5). The darkness couldn't prevail against the light.

2

The Abiding Word

If ye abide in me, and my words abide in you, ye shall ask what ye will, and it shall be done unto you.

Herein is my Father glorified, that ye bear much fruit; so shall ye be my disciples.

John 15:7,8

Notice, the Word must abide in you for you to bear fruit and glorify God.

Then again in John 14:23 notice He said:

. . . If a man love me, he will keep my words: and my Father will love him, and we (not just me, but we — the Father, the Son, and the Holy Ghost) will come unto him, and make our abode with him.

If you love Him, you will keep His Word in your temple, for your body is the temple of the Holy Ghost. Your human spirit is housed in this temple. Keep the Word in your human spirit, and Jesus will make His abode with you!

The abiding Word in your human spirit will create a lifestyle fit for God; then the Father, the Son, and the Holy Spirit will set up camp inside you!

Many people say, "I just never know what to do when bad situations arise. I'm always in the wrong place at the wrong time. I'm never where I ought to be." They go on repeating what the devil told them.

They have overdosed on the devil's word. They need to try to overdose on *God's Word* instead of talking the devil's language.

You can tell instantly when the Word of God *abides in them.* That Word will cause them to speak in line with what God said about them: "Whatever I do will prosper. No weapon formed against me shall prosper. I'm always in the right place at the right time!"

God's image of you is perfected by speaking God's Word after Him. The Word enlightens your innermost being. Your head may be screaming, "You dummy! It's not so! You're lying! You're never in the right place!" Sometimes you might not be, but *you should continually affirm what God said about you regardless of what you are experiencing.*

The Word says that no weapon formed against you shall prosper and whatever you do will prosper, so even your mistakes will prosper if you believe for it! It's the Word on your lips, coming out of your mouth, that causes your candle to give light. (Is. 54:17; Ps. 1:3; 119:130.)

In Psalm 19:14, David said, **Let the words of my mouth, and the meditation of my heart, be acceptable in thy sight, O Lord . . . .** This is what God wants us to do: speak only words that are acceptable to Him.

Many things acceptable to God are unacceptable to religious people. Some don't want to hear or see what is pleasing to God.

3

God Wants
to Reveal Mysteries

Let's take a look at the attitude of Jesus concerning those who don't want to see or hear the truth.

> And the disciples came, and said unto him, Why speakest thou unto them in parables?

> He answered and said unto them, Because it is given unto you to know the mysteries of the kingdom of heaven, but to them it is not given.

> For whosoever hath, to him shall be given, and he shall have more abundance: but whosoever hath not, from him shall be taken away even that he hath.

> Therefore speak I to them in parables: because they seeing see not; and hearing they hear not, neither do they understand.

And in them is fulfilled the prophecy
of Esaias, which saith, By hearing ye shall
hear, and shall not understand; and seeing ye shall see, and shall not perceive:

For this people's heart is waxed gross,
and their ears are dull of hearing, and
their eyes they have closed; lest at any
time they should see with their eyes, and
hear with their ears, and should understand with their heart, and should be con-
verted, and I should heal them.

Matthew 13:10-15

Notice Jesus said, . . . **their eyes *they*
have closed.**   *It was an act of their wills.*
The word *closed* is the same Greek word
from which we get our English word
squinted.   The Word brought the light of
truth to them, and they squinted or
closed their eyes to that light.   They were
accustomed to darkness.

Jesus said, . . . **lest at any time they
should see with their eyes, and hear with
their ears, and should understand with
their heart . . . and I should heal them.**
If the Word had entered their heart, they
would have been healed and delivered,
but they would not receive it.

If you have been in a dark room for a long time, you will squint when the door is opened into the sunlight. Because your eyes have become adjusted to darkness, they react to sudden light.

That is what Jesus was referring to, but He goes on to say, **. . . blessed are your eyes, for they see: and your ears, for they hear.** The human spirit is capable of receiving God's Word that brings great light and wisdom.

In 1 Corinthians 1:30 Paul says Jesus is made unto us wisdom, righteousness, sanctification, and redemption. Jesus was the Word made flesh. He *is* the light of men. He was the Word of God in physical form, performing the work of the Word on earth. He healed the sick, raised the dead, and cast out demons to show us what God's Word could do on earth.

Jesus died, was resurrected, and ascended to the Father, but the Word is still with us to heal and deliver. The Word works the same today. The Apostle Paul tapped into it when he said, **. . . the righteousness which is of faith**

speaketh on this wise . . . The word is nigh thee, even in thy mouth, and in thy heart: that is, the word of faith, which we preach (Rom. 10:6,8).

This is one way God will light your candle: *with His Word.* His Word will enlighten you. Speak it out of your mouth and it will get into your spirit. Then it will bring results. Many people are trying to operate with a head knowledge of the Word, but it won't work when you only have a head knowledge. It must be a revelation in your spirit.

Notice Proverbs 18:14: **The spirit of a man will sustain his infirmity; but a wounded spirit who can bear?** The human spirit will *sustain his infirmity.* A footnote in my Bible says it will *hold in* or *hold off* his infirmity. This sheds a different light on it, doesn't it? The human spirit will *sustain, hold in,* or *hold off* an infirmity.

Speaking the devil's words will cause your spirit to hold an infirmity in you. Speaking God's Word will cause your spirit to hold off an infirmity from you.

When God's Word is conceived in the human spirit, the Holy Spirit has something to work with. *It is the Word and the Spirit that brings the manifestation of God's power.* Some people have the Spirit but no Word for the Spirit to work with. Others have the Word but not the Spirit. But it takes both to have the manifestation of God's power.

4
Words Can Establish Circumstances

Proverbs 18:20 says, **A man's belly shall be satisfied with the fruit of his mouth; and with the increase of his lips shall he be filled.**

Now take into consideration what Paul said in Romans 10: **. . . the righteousness which is of faith speaketh on this wise . . . . The word is nigh thee, even in thy mouth, and in thy heart . . .** (vv. 6,8). Paul's statement seems to amplify Proverbs 18:20: **A man's belly shall be satisfied with the fruit of his mouth . . . .**

I believe the word *belly* is referring to the human spirit or heart of man. It will be satisfied with what you say. It will either *hold in* the infirmity (weakness, sickness) or *hold it off*. **And with the increase of his lips shall he be filled.** In other words, he will be filled with what he speaks. You will also be filled with what you speak: good or bad, blessing or curse.

Let's say a situation arises and you need several thousand dollars. What do you say? The righteousness which is of faith says, "The Word is near me — in my mouth and in my heart."

So your spirit man asks, "What does the Word say?"

In Philippians it says that your God shall supply all your need according to His riches in glory — IF you have given like the Philippian church gave.

But you look around and see lack. What are you going to establish with your words: present circumstances of lack or the promise of abundance from God's Word?

Remember, you will be filled with the increase of your lips. And if the Word does not abide in you, you will establish your present circumstances by your own words.

This is why God told Joshua, "Don't let the Book of the Law depart out of your mouth." (Josh. 1:8.) That was the Word of God in Joshua's day. God knew Joshua would be filled with the increase of his lips.

God gives us great insight into this in Proverbs 18:21: **Death and life are in the power of the tongue: and they that love it shall eat the fruit thereof.**

Let me mention something here that you may not have thought about. Since death and life are in the power of the tongue, *you can speak death to the words of the devil* by resisting him with God's Word. For the Word of God is quick and powerful, sharper than any two-edged sword. Speak life by speaking God's Word! For death and life are in the power of the tongue! Whatever you speak life to is what you establish. But *you must make the decision!* Which will you speak life to — God's Word or the devil's?

Regardless of what God promises you in His Word, if that promise doesn't get inside you, you will never be enlightened to it. You may hear it outwardly and know that it's in the Bible; but the most effective method for getting God's Word implanted into your spirit is to speak it into your heart. As God told Joshua: *Don't let it depart out of your mouth. Keep it in your mouth day and night.*

In Proverbs 3:3 we find this statement: **Write them upon the table of thine heart.** How can you write on the table of your heart? David gives us insight into this: **My tongue is the pen of a ready writer** (Ps. 45:1). You write these things in your heart with your tongue. Man's belly (spirit) will be satisfied with the fruit of his mouth. Your spirit will receive and be satisfied with what you speak, whether right or wrong.

James 1:26 says, **If any man among you seem to be religious, and bridleth not his tongue, but deceiveth his own heart . . . .** Your words will deceive your spirit into believing what you are saying is what you want.

That is the reason words are so important. You should never speak anything that disagrees with the Word of God. God's Word is the final authority.

Whether it looks like it is true or regardless of what you think, God's Word is still the final authority.

What you think is not going to change God's Word, but your thoughts *will change* the *effect of His Word on you.* The point I want to drive home is: **God wants to light your candle!** He wants to bring light into your spirit. The entrance of His Word does truly bring light.

In Psalm 17:4, David makes this statement: **Concerning the works of men, by the word of thy lips I have kept me from the paths of the destroyer.** He said, "Father, by the words of Your lips, I have kept myself from the paths of the destroyer."

Keep Yourself

This brings up another scripture. Whosoever is born of God keeps himself, and the wicked one touches him not. (1 John 5:18.) Sometimes we leave everything up to God. We say, "I believe God is going to take care of this situation. I'll just leave it up to Him." But John said, he that is born of God keepeth himself from the wicked one.

You may ask, "How do you keep yourself from the wicked one?"

David gives us the answer in Psalm 17:4. He says, *"By the word of thy lips* (God's lips) *I keep me* (or myself) *from the paths of the destroyer."* In other words, he is saying to God, "I have taken the words of Your lips . . . ." The indication is that he put them in his mouth. The Word of God enlightened David's spirit until *he began to see things the way God saw them.*

Seeing the Way God Sees

One of the major problems in the Body of Christ today is that so many see themselves as the devil sees them, not as God sees them. If we are to be victorious, we must get the image of God inside us and see ourselves the way God sees us.

God sees us as He said we were: *victorious.* **. . . whatsoever is born of God overcometh the world: and this is the victory that overcometh the world, even**

our faith (1 John 5:4).   **Beloved,** *now* **are we the sons of God** (1 John 3:2).

We will not become the sons of God when we get to heaven.   We are sons of God *now.*   If we aren't sons of God here, we won't make it to heaven.   We must have within us the image that God has of us, then we will be enlightened and see that God's fullness will dwell in us as we keep His Word.

5
Words Create Images

With God's words you can create His image of you. The more of His words you use, the more you will have a clearer image.

I could tell you about the airplane the ministry owns. It's a single-engine plane. That gives a certain image. It's tan and red with brown stripes. Now you have a better image. If I told you its registration number, you could go to the airport and locate it without ever having seen it.

You could point to it and say, "That's it!" Why? Because that's the image I built in you with words. I created a video in your mind by a proper sequence of words concerning my airplane. Words affect you that way by perfecting the image.

This is why Jesus said, "Take heed what you hear." (Mark 4:24.) You don't need to hear all the things the devil has said because his words also create images. Jesus made this powerful statement as He spoke to Satan: "Man shall not live by bread alone, but by *every Word of God.*" (Matt. 4:4.)

Reciprocal Truth

There is also a reciprocal to this truth: If man shall live by every Word of God, then man will die by the words of the devil! If you speak God's Word, it will impart God's life to you. If you speak the negative things the enemy says about you, those words will bring defeat, doubt, unbelief, and can eventually cause spiritual death.

Man shall live by *every Word of God.* Why? Because there is life in every Word of God. As Jesus said in John 6:63, **. . . the words that I speak unto you, they are spirit, and they are life.**

There is still Spirit life in the words that Jesus spoke. He imparted the Spirit that was in Him into every word He spoke. The words He spoke can impart that same Spirit life to you!

If you can live by the Word of God, then you can die by the words of the devil. The negative words of the enemy will bring death, for the world is moving in a negative stream. If Jesus' words impart Spirit life, then the words of the devil impart spirit death. *The spirit Satan imparts in words brings destruction.*

Take Heed Who You Hear

Words make a tremendous impression on the human spirit. Be careful who you follow after and who you fellowship with on a consistent basis.

I have heard people say, "Yes, I know that person is off base in a few areas. But I'm like an old cow — smart enough to eat the hay and spit out the sticks!"

But let me tell you a true story about a horse we had. This horse was eating hay every day, but one day we noticed she wouldn't eat a thing. This went on for several days so we called the veterinarian, and he came to examine the horse. He looked in her mouth, then he ran his arm into her mouth almost up to his elbow and pulled out a stick that had been stuck there. That stick was causing so much pain that she couldn't eat anything.

The bottom line is that sometimes you can't spit out sticks. If they get "hung in your throat," you won't be able to receive anything from anyone!

6
Job's Revelation

There are many things in the Book of Job that people don't understand. But if you really study it, you will find that much of it is prophetic. The Book of Job contains some astounding revelations.

> Moreover Job continued his parable, and said,
>
> Oh that I were as in months past, as in the days when God preserved me;
>
> *When his candle shined upon my head,* and when by his light I walked through darkness;
>
> As I was in the days of my youth, when the secret of God was upon my tabernacle.

Job 29:1-4

I believe this chapter is also prophetic of Jesus by law of double reference. . . . **When his candle shined upon my**

39

**head, and when by his light I walked
through darkness . . . .**

Under the Old Covenant, the Holy
Spirit was only upon the prophets,
priests, and kings. We have a better
Covenant today: as believers today we
have the Holy Spirit abiding in us! This
is why Job makes this statement: **When
his candle shined** *upon* **my head.** Notice
it wasn't *in him*, it was *upon his head.*

In the Scriptures we read that the
Holy Spirit came *upon them.* They were
not baptized in the Holy Spirit as we are
today. But He came upon them.

**. . . As I was in the days of my youth,
when the secret of God was** *upon* **my
tabernacle.** Notice again, it's *upon*, not
in.

When Jesus talked about the Spirit of
Truth that would come, He said, "He will
guide you into all truth. He will teach
you things to come." The Spirit of Truth,
or the Spirit of Christ as He is called, will
teach and guide you. In other words, He
will enlighten you.

Revelation
Within the Human Spirit

The Holy Spirit dwells in the human spirit. The human spirit is capable of receiving the things of God. This is how Paul put it in 1 Corinthians 2:7-9:

> But we speak the wisdom of God in a mystery, even the hidden wisdom, which God ordained before the world unto our glory:

> Which none of the princes of this world knew: for had they known it, they would not have crucified the Lord of glory.

> But as it is written, Eye hath not seen, nor ear heard, neither have entered into the heart of man, the things which God hath prepared for them that love him.

Some people read this and say, "Yes. You know the Bible says nobody knows . . ." *But we do have access* to that knowledge *if we read the next verse.*

> But God hath revealed them unto us by his Spirit: for the Spirit searcheth all things, yea, the deep things of God (v. 10).

What Spirit searches *all* things? In the *King James Version*, the word *spirit* is capitalized, but I don't believe Paul is referring to the Holy Spirit. I believe he is referring to the human spirit.

Ask yourself this question: "Why would the Holy Spirit need to search the things of God?" *The Holy Spirit already knows the things of God.* I believe it is the human spirit that searches the things of God. No person can be truly fulfilled in life unless their spirit is in tune with God's Spirit. The human spirit is always in search of true happiness and fulfillment that comes only by being in fellowship with our Father, God.

Notice again verse 9: **Eye hath not seen . . . neither have entered into the heart of man . . . .** That seems to be a contradiction because the next verse says, **But God hath revealed them unto us by his Spirit.** It *did* enter into the heart, but it came by the Holy Spirit into the human spirit. God enlightens us through our human spirit. *There is no contradiction here* for it did not come by sense knowledge but by revelation to the heart.

Paul said, "Compare spiritual things with spiritual." First, he reveals the fact that the natural eye has not seen, the

natural ear has not heard, neither has it
entered into the heart of man *through the
five senses.* It did not come by seeing,
hearing, smelling, tasting, or feeling.
God revealed it to us by His Spirit. It
came by the Spirit of God into our human
spirits.

Light Your Candle!

God wants to light your candle and
enlighten your darkness. But the candle
of the wicked shall be put out. (Prov.
24:20.)

Now you hear the world say this:
"Well, they're burning the candle at both
ends!" Yes, that's a different candle!

If God lights your *spiritual* candle, you
won't have to burn the *carnal* candle at
both ends. You will be in the right place
at the right time and know the right thing
to do. God will lead you by your spirit
to the right business deal. He will reveal
it to you days, weeks, or months in
advance. He will teach you things to
come so you can travel His road to
success.

Let It Burn!

When your candle is burning, God will lead you by your spirit. The things you can't see with your natural eye, He will reveal to your spirit. He will say, "No! Don't bid on that deal. You'll get into trouble!"

You say, "But I don't see anything bad about it. Everybody thinks it's good. It really seems to be the thing to do." Then down in your spirit the red light comes on! Something there says, "No! Don't do it!"

Have you ever walked up to someone and had that red light inside you begin to flash? Your spirit seems to draw up in a knot. You hear, "Be careful! Don't get involved with this guy. There is darkness here. Things aren't as they seem."

You say, "But I don't see a thing wrong with him."

You had better listen to that voice inside you. That's your candle burning. Let God enlighten you. Remember: **The spirit of man is the candle of the**

Lord, searching all the inward parts of the belly.

I'm convinced that if we would develop ourselves to be led by the Spirit and allow the candle of the Lord to enlighten us, *we would be a success in everything we set out to do.*

But we must train ourselves to listen to our spirit.

You may say, "I don't understand how my spirit can do that." You don't have to understand all about it. You can know things beyond what the natural mind can understand. You can be in the right place at the right time when you are enlightened by your spirit.

Get your mouth in agreement with God's Word by confessing: "Whatever I do will prosper! No weapon formed against me shall prosper!"

Psalm 112:4 says, **Unto the upright there ariseth light in the darkness.** Now I'm sure you realize that the world is getting darker every day. But it's not something Christians should get discouraged about and want to hide in the mountains about, *for light shall arise in you, even in the midst of darkness!*

Someone might say, "How in the world do you think you are going to have so much light when everyone else is walking in darkness?" Because your candle is burning! God's Word is a lamp unto your feet and a light unto your path.

7

Walking in the Light

Things are not going to get better in the world. The world will be walking further into darkness, stumbling as they go. But you don't have to stumble in darkness. You can have the light of life.

As we approach the end of the age, we as believers are coming closer to the Kingdom of Light. That makes our light grow brighter. But as unbelievers the world is getting closer to the kingdom of darkness. Therefore their darkness will grow darker because their lamp is put out.

When Adam was created by God and put on earth, his candle (spirit) was burning. The Holy Spirit enlightened him through his spirit. But when he sinned, his candle went out; then he was ruled totally by his five senses.

Candle-Lighting Ceremony

Every man after Adam was ruled by his physical senses until the Day of Pentecost when there was a candle-lighting ceremony. In the Upper Room, 120 candles were lit; then before the day was over, their number had grown to over 3,000! *That was a candle-lighting ceremony second to none!* They could *then* receive and understand the Word of God.

Have you noticed in the Scriptures that when Jesus told the disciples exactly what was going to happen to Him, they just stood there as if to say, "Huh?" (That's Arkansas talk for *What?*) When He told them He was to be crucified and die, they said, "When You set up Your kingdom here in Jerusalem, we want to sit beside You." They didn't understand a thing He said.

But when they were born again, they called to remembrance the things He had said because their spirits had come alive to the things of God. His words then became understandable. Their candles were burning — light had come!

Secret of God

Let's look again at Job's words: **As I was in the days of my youth, when the secret of God was *upon* my tabernacle . . .** (Job 29:4).   Notice he said *upon it*, not *in it*.   You will notice a difference between the language used in the Old Covenant and the New Testament.

In John 14:16,17 Jesus said:

And I will pray the Father, and he shall give you another Comforter, that he may abide with you for ever;

Even the Spirit of truth; whom the world cannot receive, because it seeth him not, neither knoweth him: but ye know him; for he dwelleth with you, *and shall be in you*.

Under the New Covenant the Holy Spirit comes to abide in your human spirit and bring revelation.   He reveals things to your spirit that don't come by the five physical senses.   They are revealed to you from within.

In 1 Corinthians 2:12 Paul makes this statement: **Now we have received, not the spirit of the world, but the spirit which is of God; that we might know the**

things that are freely given to us of God.
What spirit did we receive?   The human
spirit which is of God.

He is telling you that God has
imparted His Spirit to you.   Why?   So
you can know the things that are freely
given to you of God and not have to walk
in darkness, so you won't have to say:
"Eye hath not seen nor ear heard, nobody
knows what God has done."   Yes, we do
know for He has revealed them by His
Holy Spirit into our human spirits.

Comparing Spiritual Things

The spirit of man is truly the candle
of the Lord.   It's the means God uses to
enlighten us so we might know the things
freely given to us of God, which things
also we speak not in words which man's
wisdom teaches, but which the Holy
Ghost teaches, *comparing spiritual things
with spiritual*.   (1 Cor. 2:12,13.)

Here Paul is referring to the human
spirit for that's the spiritual part of man.
Your physical body doesn't have an ounce
of spirituality in it!   The change starts in
your human spirit and changes you from

within. But the natural man receives not the things of the Spirit of God for they are foolishness to him, *neither can he know them, because they are spiritually discerned.* (v. 14.)

Tapping the Source of Knowledge

The natural man — your physical body and mind — doesn't know all about you, but God's Spirit and your spirit do. Notice Paul's statement: **. . . what man knoweth the things of a man, save the spirit of man which is in him? even so the things of God knoweth no man, but the Spirit of God** (1 Cor. 2:11).

This reveals that the human spirit knows all about you, and the Spirit of God knows all about God. So when you bring those two spirits together, *you have tapped the Source of all knowledge.* In other words, *you've got your candle lit!* The light is turned on in your spirit.

But he that is spiritual judgeth all things . . . (1 Cor. 2:15). Now, who is he that is spiritual? It's the spirit man (human spirit) on the inside of you that is spiritual, and he judges all things. But

your spirit is judged by no man. Men
may judge your actions, but they can't
judge your spirit — only God can do that.

8

The Mind of Christ

For who hath known the mind of the Lord, that he may instruct him? But we have the mind of Christ (1 Cor. 2:16). *How* do we have the mind of Christ? Through the Word of God and the human spirit, for God's Spirit bears witness with our spirits. When the human spirit and God's Spirit come into unity, we are in contact with the Source of all knowledge.

Let Your Lights Burn

Now let's go to Luke's Gospel and see something Jesus said that will shed more light on this subject.

> But rather seek ye the kingdom of God; and all these things shall be added unto you.

> Fear not, little flock; for it is your Father's good pleasure to give you the kingdom.

Sell that ye have, and give alms; provide yourselves bags which wax not old, a treasure in the heavens that faileth not, where no thief approacheth, neither moth corrupteth.

For where your treasure is, there will your heart be also.

Luke 12:31-34

Treasure in the Heart

In other words, your treasure is in your heart.

Now notice verse 35: **Let your loins be girded about, and your lights burning.** Your loins are to be girded with truth. The Word of God is the truth that you are to be girded with, and the "lights" He is referring to is your spirit.

Turn the Light On

Good advice: Gird yourself with the Word and let your lights burn. When you are girded with the Word, your candle is bright. God's Word will enlighten you to the wisdom of God, to the mind and direction of the Spirit of God. The Word is the fuel supply for the light.

Yea, the light of the wicked shall be put out, and the spark of his fire shall not shine.

The light shall be dark in his tabernacle, and his candle shall be put out with him.

Job 18:5,6

The light of the righteous rejoiceth: but the lamp of the wicked shall be put out.

Proverbs 13:9

What does all this mean?

I believe that as the wicked come closer to the end and refuse the light of the Word, their darkness will grow darker. Even what little light they have received from others will be put out.

Even in the business world, I believe those who have had the knowledge to make millions will lose it in the days to come, *unless* they get their candles lit.

For there shall be no reward to the evil man; the candle of the wicked shall be put out (Prov. 24:20).

Recompensed in the Earth

The righteous shall be recompensed in the earth: much more the wicked and the sinner (Prov. 11:31). I believe Proverbs 8:12 is prophetic of inventions that will come in our day through men of God who are enlightened by God's Spirit: **I wisdom dwell with prudence, and find out knowledge of witty inventions.** Verse 18 says, **Riches and honour are with me; yea, durable riches and righteousness.**

When wisdom dwells with prudence, it is capable of producing inventions that will bring durable riches and righteousness. Many of them have already come on the scene. Some will astound the world! Some will be used to preach the Gospel to the world. Others, I believe, will be used during the Millennium.

God has some great things in store for us in this age. But if you are not living for God, if you don't put the Word of God in your heart, your candle will be put out. For darkness, even gross darkness, shall cover the earth in the days to come; and

without the lamp of the Lord, you will
have no guide, and confusion will be the
rule of the day.

But there is good news for you! Your
spirit is the candle of the Lord, *so you can
have the light of life!* God will enlighten
your darkness if you will commit your life
to Him.

**The path of the just is as the shining
light, that shineth more and more unto
the perfect day** (Prov. 4:18). Notice the
path of the just is **as the shining light that
shineth more and more.** In other words,
it's getting *brighter!*

But **the way of the wicked is as
darkness: they know not at what they
stumble** (Prov. 4:19). And we are coming closer to that day. God has given the
five-fold ministry — apostles, prophets,
evangelists, pastors, teachers — for the
perfecting of the saints, for the work of
the ministry, for the edifying of the Body
of Christ until we all come to the unity
of faith and the knowledge of the Son of
God, unto a *perfect man,* unto the measure
of the stature of the fullness of Christ.
(Eph. 4:11,12.)

Those who make a decision to walk in this light, then their pathway will be a way of light. But the wicked will go further and further into darkness and confusion. Proverbs 11:8 shall be proven true: **The righteous is delivered out of trouble, and the wicked cometh in his stead.**

I believe in the days to come the wicked will become more confused and lose what insight they have in this world system. But the righteous will grow in wisdom and understanding of God's ways.

But those who are not enlightened by the light of life will stumble in the darkness. It is that darkness that will bring fear upon mankind. **The fear of the wicked, it shall come upon him: but the desire of the righteous shall be granted** (Prov. 10:24). **The integrity of the upright shall guide them: but the perverseness of transgressors shall destroy them** (Prov. 11:3). It is plain that there is no hope for those who do not have the light of life.

If you are not born again, your heart must be changed. *You must be born again* and become a new creature in Christ. Then God's Spirit can bear witness with your spirit, for **. . . the path of the just is as the shining light, that shineth more and more unto the perfect day** (Prov. 4:18).

If you have not committed your life to Christ, do it today. For in Him is the life you have been looking for, and it is *the* light, the *true light*, that lighteth every man.

Charles Capps is a former farmer and land developer who travels throughout the United States, teaching and preaching the truths of God's Word. He shares from practical, first-hand experience how Christians can apply the Word to the circumstances of life and live victoriously.

Besides authoring several books, including the best-selling *The Tongue, A Creative Force,* Charles also has a nationwide radio ministry called "Concepts of Faith."

Charles and his wife Peggy make their home in England, Arkansas. Both their daughters, Annette and Beverly, are involved in the ministry.

For a complete list of tapes and books by Charles Capps, or to receive his publication, *Concepts of Faith*, write:

Charles Capps Ministries
P. O. Box 69
England, AR 72046

Please include your prayer requests and comments when you write.

Books by Charles Capps

Kicking Over Sacred Cows
(New pocket size!)

Dynamics of Faith and Confession

Hope — A Partner To Faith

Seedtime and Harvest

God's Image of You

Angels

Success Motivation Through The Word

The Tongue — A Creative Force

*Releasing The Ability of God
Through Prayer*

Authority In Three Worlds

*Changing The Seen
and
Shaping The Unseen*

Can Your Faith Fail?

How You Can Avoid Tragedy

*God's Creative Power
Will Work For You*
(also available in Spanish)

How To Have Faith In Your Faith

NEW: *The Light of Life
In the Spirit of Man*

Available from your local bookstore.

Harrison House
P. O. Box 35035 • Tulsa, OK 74153